Noor upon Noor

Collection of Muslim Quotes.

Written by s.hukr

Noor upon Noor

Publisher: Fajr Noor © 2024

All Rights Reserved

ISBN: 9780645349962

Designed & Authored by s.hukr

Website: fajrnoor.com

Noor upon Noor

Salam.

I hope you find peace, wisdom and love through these words. I hope this book inspires you to love yourself, educate yourself and become a better Muslim.

May Allah guide you towards that which is best while making your Dunya and your Deen easy for you.

If there is a word that you do not understand, simply search the definition of the word on Google.com.

e.g. "Define [word]"

fajrnoor.com.au

Noor upon Noor

You must first become knowledgeable then you must become wise.

For when you have wisdom, you don't have doubts. You don't have insecurities.

You know exactly what is what, even if the whole world says something else.

s.hukr

Noor upon Noor

I see our men struggle with Salah and
I see our women struggle with Hijab.

I see our parents struggle with marriage
and our children struggle with mental health.

We struggle with basic things because
we live our life not according to Islam,
but according to cultural & social norms.

s.hukr

Noor upon Noor

Let me remind you by saying that there is no such thing as feminism in Islam. Allah perfected Islam 1400 years ago.

Women were given their rights long before feminism was ever introduced to this world.

s.hukr

Noor upon Noor

I don't know about you, but I would rather have Noor on my face than have money on the table.

I would rather be in love, have divine knowledge and be close to my lord than have the temporary luxuries of this world.

This world is meaningless. It is temporary. It is a place of problems, trials, tribulations. It is not my Paradise and it will never be.

s.hukr

Noor upon Noor

People make dua and expect
things to fall from the sky.

That is not how you make dua.
That is not how you worship Allah.

s.hukr

Noor upon Noor

This world was not made for you and I.
We don't belong here; we will never fit in
and call this place our home.

As soon as the dust settles and we become
comfortable, a fire erupts from places we least
expect it and we are reminded that the peace
of this world is temporary.

s.hukr

Noor upon Noor

Be authentic. Be real.
Notice how I didn't say to be perfect.

People value authenticity, they value those who stay true to themselves even if the world hates them or doesn't agree with them.

Stop caring about what others think about you. Stop trying to please everyone. Your job isn't to satisfy anyone except God.

s.hukr

Noor upon Noor

"Iqra!"

The first word revealed by Allah.

"Read" does not mean recite.
Allah didn't say recite, he said "Read".

Read means to comprehend and understand.

To understand, we must use the intellect Allah gave us. Don't read God's words blindly, understand them and live by them.

s.hukr

Noor upon Noor

Hijab is not only a headscarf that women must wear. It is the practice of Haya and Haya is the companion of Iman.

s.hukr

"Indeed, Haya and Iman are Companions. When one of them is lifted, the other leaves as well."
– Baihaqi

Noor upon Noor

Hijab of the Tongue:

You have a duty to protect your tongue
from foul words, gossiping and lies.

Everything you speak about,
should be with Haya.

The way you speak about people should not
be sexualised, that is not respect. Do not make
jokes that hurt people, that is not humour.

Do not lie to satisfy people, that is not Islam.
Protect your tongue against harming others.

s.hukr

Noor upon Noor

Hijab of the Eyes:

By staring at anything inappropriate, your eyes commit Zina. There is a reason why as Muslims we must lower our gaze.

It is so we can protect our soul from its lustful desires. Be aware that Allah sees everything that you see, so lower your gaze.

s.hukr

Noor upon Noor

Hijab of the Hands:

Do not allow your hands to do injustice to others or to yourself. Do not steal what is not yours. Do not assault an innocent person. Do not allow anyone to be harassed in front of you. Do not smuggle drugs, do not do them. Do not smoke sheesha, cigarettes or vapes.

They aren't good for your soul, nor will they help you on Yaumul Qiyamah. Allah is always watching you… remember that.

s.hukr

Noor upon Noor

Age doesn't mean much, character does.

You can have a 30 year old who is immature and childish, or you can have a 15 year old who knows exactly what he is doing and in complete control of his emotions
and way of life.

Age is just a measure of how long you have lived but not how much you have learned, experienced and endured life.

s.hukr

Noor upon Noor

We all go through hardship, but some of us are grateful, we have Sabr even when we have the right to complain.

We learn lessons, we subconsciously grow into the best version of ourselves. Because we know someone else has it worse than us.

We feel Alhamdulilah. We are thankful and grateful for even the trials and tests that we endure.

This is the attitude and mindset of the successful.

s.hukr

Noor upon Noor

Hand in Marriage.

There is a way to ask for someone's hand in marriage.

No, we do not flirt and play with people's hearts in the name of love and then think about marriage. We do not spend time with the opposite gender aimlessly.

This ummah is built on respect and dignity. We show this respect by seeking the approval of one's family. There is nothing wrong with a woman proposing and there is nothing wrong with rejecting a proposal as long as it is within the guidelines of Islam.

Race, age, height, hijab, status, and job title doesn't really matter. Prioritise their deen, their character, their manners, their ability to perform as a future mother/father.

If there is someone whom you like, always seek the counsel of someone because love often makes us blind. Then tell your family and their family. Meet each other under supervision of a mahram and if it's meant to be, Alhamdulillah and if not Alhamdulillah.

s.hukr

Noor upon Noor

Islam has made it clear that
forced marriages are forbidden.

That education is compulsory for
every Muslim regardless of gender.

Women in Islam are given the right to work,
to trade and earn such that her earnings are
her own and that it is the duty of the Muslim
man to provide all the necessities of life.

s.hukr

Noor upon Noor

I don't like fan girls.

I don't mind people that show me love for the sake of Allah, but I don't like the idea that people love me more than they should.

Such people will compromise their Haya, create unrealistic fantasies in their head and become emotional for the sake of creation.

I suggest you stop being a "fan girl", a seeker of attention and temporary love. It always ends in heartbreak.

I recommend that you fill the void in your life with the love of Islam, understand your true purpose of being a Muslimah, live like a Queen should.

s.hukr

Noor upon Noor

If your way of dawah is pushing
people away from Islam.

Then you are the problem.

Not Islam.

s.hukr

Noor upon Noor

Facilitating Haram is Haram.

As Muslims we do not support haram things especially when it can be avoided. We do not facilitate haram, we discourage it without being judgemental.

This means that we do not work for a place that sells alcohol, pork or forbidden goods/services such as Riba.

We do not support immodest fashion brands that promote Tabarruj. We do not support people who gossip, curse or disrespect someone in front of you.

We do not help friends get into a haram relationship or support an existing relationship of such nature. We do not support people or places that go against the teachings of Islam.

We don't judge them either, publicly harass others, we just keep our distance and do our duty.

s.hukr

Noor upon Noor

My Dear Sister,

There is a difference between being beautiful and being seductive.

Being beautiful isn't a sin but being sexually arousing in public is a sin.

s.hukr

Noor upon Noor

Don't speak about something
you don't know.

It's okay to say, 'I don't know'
or 'I lack the knowledge to
talk about this'.

s.hukr

Noor upon Noor

The closer you get to Allah the more you
will find your world revolving around Islam.

The way you speak, your dress code,
your morals, the way you think,
even the way you eat will align with Islam.

Islam isn't just a religion,
it is an ideal way of life.

It is how to live life to the fullest. It is a just
system of laws, regulations, standards and
ideas that are far superior than the
democracies of this world.

Its education is more beneficial than
universities that take away your money,
your peace and your passion.

Islam is beautiful, I hope more
people study the beauty of it.

s.hukr

Noor upon Noor

"Verily with hardship comes ease."

Don't get lost in your pain that you
forget about the cure that is promised.

Believing the cure will come
is half the medicine.

s.hukr

Noor upon Noor

When you find yourself commuting to work or school, waiting for Salah to begin at the mosque, in those precious moments remember Allah.

Do Dhikr.

Remind your soul of the reality of your existence. The purpose of your life.

Because at any moment you can taste death. At any moment Allah can take away your blessings, just because you forgot about Him.

Remember Allah and He will remember you and if you don't remember Him, He might take away your blessings, so you may remember Him again.

s.hukr

Noor upon Noor

I could never imagine cheating on anyone.
It's the type of mistake and wrongdoing
I couldn't live with.

Knowing that you destroyed someone's
trust is bad but destroying someone's
perspective on love is a crime against
humanity.

s.hukr

Noor upon Noor

I've always told people to respect their parents, to be kind to them.

But some parents need a reminder that when they fail in their duty as parents, they will meet consequences.

Parents who love too much or love too little, will end up neglecting their children and will often meet their consequences later in life.

Allah raised the status of parents in Islam but that doesn't mean you neglect your duty upon your children.

Children also have rights in Islam. If you neglect them you will face consequences.

s.hukr

Noor upon Noor

When I see this sad generation,

I don't blame them.
I look at their parents first.

Are they raising them with
culture or religion?

s.hukr

Noor upon Noor

Social media is a place full of lies because the majority of us only show a certain side of life.

Mostly the good, pretty, and perfect side. Completely hiding the pain, struggles and imperfections we go through.

I dislike how everything is so driven towards a fake and manipulated reality.

Girls with filters and excessive makeup so they always look picture perfect. Guys with perfect hair styles and displays of wealth, I think you get the idea.

Even on Instagram, your feed is catered towards your likes, not your dislikes. They feed you content that just stimulates your dopamine levels.

So you spend more time comparing yourself to a fake perception of reality.

s.hukr

Noor upon Noor

Reflect daily. Bring closure to your day through 10 minutes of reflection.

Ask yourself:

"Did I pray all my Salah?"

"What went well, what didn't?"

"What needs improvement?"

"What's stopping me from improving?"

"Am I being the best I can be?"

"If death came tomorrow, would I be ready?"

"Am I reaching my goals?"

s.hukr

Noor upon Noor

You must pray 5 times.
Because you are Muslim.

Image death came tomorrow.
And you didn't pray.
What a nightmare.

You would be lowered into your
grave being a Kafir.

s.hukr

Noor upon Noor

Some people need a mute button.

Speak only when you feel that your words are better than your silence because hell is filled with people who couldn't control their tongues.

Everything you say is written by angels on your shoulders, do not allow your tongue to be the reason why you suffer in the hereafter.

s.hukr

Noor upon Noor

I actually hate culture.

In some cultures, it's rude to come early. In some cultures, it's okay to open a door without knocking. In some cultures, people have to fight to pay the dinner bill. In some cultures, yelling is normal and being quiet is seen as being shy.

In some cultures, men don't cook or clean, they just work and make money. In some cultures, husband and wife do 50/50 split. In some cultures, haram is normalised, and halal is considered extreme religious behaviour.

But I love Islam.

It's such a peaceful and balanced way of living. It is according to Allah's instructions, what He has ordained for us. It is very beautiful, simple and easy. That's what I strive for.

But unfortunately, more than half the Muslim population follows culture not Islam.

s.hukr

Noor upon Noor

Some people are too desperate. They don't know how to let things go. They will chase people or money; they will chase temporary things. To fulfil a desire, but at what cost?

It's okay to pursue our desires and dreams but only if they are halal and the way in which we pursue them is morally acceptable.

It is okay to have the desire to be wealthy, but not through haram activities. Otherwise the desire is controlling you and you become a sinner.

Similarly, it is okay to have the desire to be beautiful, but if you perform unnecessary haram beauty treatments that go against the teachings of Islam, then you become a sinner.

s.hukr

Noor upon Noor

I've noticed that women in western societies are treated differently than those in the east.

Both cater to extremes that I don't like. Some are too liberated thus losing their value and others are too conservative that their basic rights are stripped.

I don't like either because they aren't the way of Islam. Islam is balanced, in the middle.

s.hukr

Noor upon Noor

O Women,

Your purpose isn't to dress to impress the public and then have the audacity to say men don't lower their gaze.

We all know Allah created men weak in this regard, but you aren't helping by being a makeup clown.

You need a better definition for beauty, because butterfly lashes, fake nails, caked up faces and other haram beauty treatments are not beautiful to real man.

s.hukr

Noor upon Noor

The art of being valuable comes
with a price of being hidden.

s.hukr

Noor upon Noor

Our children are our future. If you neglect them, you neglect your future. If you spoil and love them too much, you're actually doing them harm in the long term. And if you are too harsh and strict with them, they will want to distance themselves from you.

I pray that we raise a strong
future for this ummah.

s.hukr

Noor upon Noor

Islam is so beautiful that when you make Dua for someone, the angels make Dua for you.

So honour the guests of your heart.

s.hukr

Noor upon Noor

I hope one day I can leave this world
knowing that I raised a strong little
king and a brilliant young queen.

s.hukr

Noor upon Noor

On Judgement Day,

Allah isn't going to ask you how many countries you travelled too? How much money did you make? or how many goals did you achieve or did you get married?

He will simply ask; did you do what I commanded you to do?

Your soul will either tremble in fear, with regret and ending pain,

or you will in Peace.

s.hukr

Noor upon Noor

Some examples of good conduct and love between The Prophet ﷺ and his wives.

1. He would never hit his wives.
2. He would let things slide by not picking/addressing every little mistake.
3. He would play and joke around with them.
4. He would help them whenever they required help.
5. He would give them nicknames e.g. He used to call Aa'isha (ra) 'O Aa'ish' or 'Humayra' which signifies something that is small and red.
6. He would drink from the exact same part of the vessel from where his wife would drink from.
7. He would spend on them.
8. He would do things on their behalf even after their death like when he sacrificed an animal and gave some of the meat to Khadija's (ra) friends.
9. When A'a'isha (ra) was on her menstrual cycle, he would lean against her and recite Quran while they both rested.

s.hukr

Noor upon Noor

In Islam,

a Mahram is a member of one's family with whom marriage would be considered haram; from whom concealment of the body with hijab, is not obligatory; and with whom, if he is an adult male, she may be escorted during a journey, although an escort may not be obligatory.

s.hukr

Noor upon Noor

What is Mahr?

In Islam, Mahr is compulsory.

It is a form of a gift that is given by the groom to the bride at the time of Marriage.

While Mahr is often money, it can also be anything agreed upon by the bride such as jewellery, home goods, hajj or even a Quran.

It is a gift that is agreed upon by both parties. It shouldn't be too much nor too low but a reasonable amount according to one's social economic status.

s.hukr

Islam is about balance not about extremes, you should specify a low Mahr for Barakat, as the Prophet ﷺ said: "The most blessed Nikah is the one with least expenses." – Bayhaqi

Noor upon Noor

I think people don't know how to love.
Especially men. Nobody teaches us how
to love properly.

Some of us love our parents and neglect our
wives, some of us love our children and
neglect our parents. Some of us love material
things and neglect our hereafter and some of
us love Deen and neglect our Dunya.

Balance is key and is achieved when Allah is in
the centre of the heart. We must live our life
according to the Quran. We must learn how to
distribute our love equally amongst each
aspect of our life. Not pouring too much nor
pouring too little but just the right amount.

There is blessing when we follow
the ways of the Prophet ﷺ.

s.hukr

Noor upon Noor

My love once I find you, I will treasure you like a gem from the heavens because you are God's greatest gift to me.

I will move mountains for you, bring you peace after every hardship and comfort you to the best of my ability but never allow your ego to hinder my connection with God.

s.hukr

Noor upon Noor

Please stop normalising marriage amongst cousins. Amongst your own race and your own people.

I know that it is halal but there are almost 2 billion Muslims today and this ummah needs to be united.

I think Marriage is one of the ways we can create powerful bonds. The bond of marriage can unite two different families, two different bloodlines, two different countries and two different cultures.

Let us create bonds between this ummah, stop living in your toxic cultured mindset. There is nothing wrong with marrying another Muslim from a different country, culture, or family.

Actually, the Prophet did it.
So why can't you?

s.hukr

Noor upon Noor

I hope we can unite and inspire enough
change to see the children of Palestine,
Afghanistan, Uyghurs and all Muslim
nations to wake up to peace
and prosperity.

For that to happen, we must unite
under the ways of Islam.

We must let go of our ego, our
culture and our comfort zone.

s.hukr

Noor upon Noor

May Allah unite this ummah as strong as the bonds between atoms, grant us faith stronger than mountains and place in our land's protection from injustice and cruelty.

I pray this ummah comes to the
realisation that we must wake up
and do what needs to be done.

s.hukr

Noor upon Noor

I feel that Muslim women aren't
as beautiful as they once were.

No, I'm not talking about everyone but a
growing majority. I'm not talking about
outward beauty, that isn't as important
as the beauty within.

There used to be an aura glowing within
them and when you saw a glimpse
of their face, you would see Noor.

I barely see it these days.

s.hukr

Noor upon Noor

You are already physically beautiful but it's the beauty of the soul that excites another soul.

s.hukr

Noor upon Noor

I hear many girls and guys
complain about one another.

Girls complain about how there
aren't any good guys and guys
complain about the same reality.

Stop focusing on the other gender.

Focus on yourself. Because I bet half
of you struggle with the simple things
in Islam, like praying on time.

Instead of complaining and pointing out the
flaws in one another, focus on yourself so
much, in terms of personality and character,
and then watch how you attract people like a
magnet.

"Verily, Good women are for good men and
good men are for good women".

s.hukr

Noor upon Noor

Brother,

She isn't looking for riches,
beauty or poetry. She is looking
to be understood, respected and loved.

Respect is how you attract her, understanding
her will give her security and love will make
her yours forever.

Why are men of this generation
so dumb and selfish?

s.hukr

Noor upon Noor

Teach your children common sense because apparently, they don't teach that anymore.

Teach them kindness, love and tell them about the delights of Paradise. So they make that their goal in life and not money, fame or worldly success.

s.hukr

Noor upon Noor

Only guys will understand this:

Late night driving, windows down, no music,
no friends, alone, silently listening to the wind.

Moments of Peace. Clarity. And Wisdom.

s.hukr

Noor upon Noor

Allah made the Quran for us to read, to read with understanding and comprehension.

So tell me why is it on the
bookshelf collecting dust?

s.hukr

Noor upon Noor

This world is tiring.
I look forward to the day of escape.
My unappreciated soul needs rest.

s.hukr

Noor upon Noor

Ghayrah - غَيْرَة

In Islam we have a concept of Ghayrah. Ghayrah is an Arabic word which loosely translates to protective jealously.

I find it strange when I see Men who are not even embarrassed when their wives, sisters and womenfolk are all dressed up, ready to attract the attention of other men. They don't care if another man mingles with their womenfolk.

Let me remind you, that we follow Islam. And all Muslim men should have a collective sense of protectiveness for Muslim women as Allah says in the Quran: "The Men are the protectors and maintainers of women…" (Quran 4:34).

It is a major sin for a Muslim Man to not have Ghayrah. Ghayrah is a good type of jealousy, it is a natural inbuilt feeling Allah has given men and women. I personally think it is more important for men to have this feeling of jealously.

But both Muslim men and women must protect and guard one another from indecency, we should have this uneasiness in our hearts of Ghayrah, because not having it, leads to major sins.

s.hukr

Noor upon Noor

Honestly, life is full of wonders;
God makes the unthinkable happen.

We plan something but Allah has
something better planed for us.

So always trust him with your fate.
And never give up trying your best.

s.hukr

Noor upon Noor

Sometimes I get messages from complete strangers that I've never met. Paragraphs telling me how I've changed their life.

They share their story with me and it genuinely brings me joy. I find it amazing how a few words on a piece of paper can inspire people towards success. Towards happiness. Towards self-change.

I don't believe the miracle comes from me, rather it is always Allah who guides us, and this is His miracle.

My advice would be to become people who inspire goodness, don't force religion, display it in a such a beautiful manner within yourself that people would love to be your friend.

Your character becomes the reason Noor shines on your face and attracts people closer to their lord.

s.hukr

Noor upon Noor

I witness men wear short shorts,
ripped jeans and clothing that
would be inappropriate for Salah.

The same is true for the women.
Why is there an opportunity given
for people to commit Zina of the eyes?

If your clothing isn't adequate for your 5
daily prayers then you need to change
your wardrobe immediately.

s.hukr

Noor upon Noor

"Modest Fashion" is a term that gets used a lot but it's not always modest.

What is modest clothing?

Modest clothing means a piece of clothing that covers in such a way that it does not expose your adornments. It covers and does not reveal your features a in way that would seduce the opposite gender.

s.hukr

Noor upon Noor

I find it crazy how easily you can influence people, yani if I say, 'Girls who wear abayas are cute', a group of girls are now more likely to consider wearing it.

Yes, we should influence people in a positive manner, but my opinions shouldn't have more weight in your life than Islam or any other person for that matter.

Islam should always have more priority in your life than anyone's opinion unless the other persons opinion completely aligns with Islam.

s.hukr

Noor upon Noor

I hate seeing Muslims at shesha lounges or clubs. Brother go to the mosque instead, visit the house of Allah. Let go of the places where sin is common. I don't wanna see you in hell, begging for a second chance.

s.hukr

Noor upon Noor

When your parents are not rich but still afford to give you a beautiful life, please appreciate their sacrifice.

s.hukr

Noor upon Noor

Be the woman who fixes another woman's
hijab, without telling the world it was absent.

s.hukr

Noor upon Noor

I used to think all Muslims were the same.

They would all have the same set of beliefs, ideals and morals. Their opinions and mindset would align with the Quran.

However, I was very wrong.

I found out that Muslims forgot how to read the Quran. They changed read to recite, sunnah to optional, made halal difficult and haram easy.

Then they started to differentiate themselves into different categories. Liberal or traditional, Shia or Sunni. Moderate or practicing etc.

Why can't we have people with a balanced mindset. Neither east or west, nor up or down, but centred. Why can't every Muslim pick up the Quran and start reading until they understand what Allah wants them to do?

s.hukr

Noor upon Noor

Do sects exist in Islam?

No. Islam is not made up of sects.

Yes, some people have divided our religion into different "sects", but Islam is one religion perfected by Allah through the messenger of Allah, as mentioned in the Quran:

"This day have I perfected your religion for you, completed My favour upon you, and have chosen for you Islam as your religion." 5:3

We are one ummah united under God's book. We follow the teachings of the Prophet ﷺ because Allah told us to in His book.

...

Noor upon Noor

If people preach "Islam" that goes against the teachings of Quran and Sunnah, then they are answerable and held accountable by Allah.

"And if Allah had willed, He could have made you [of] one religion, but He causes to stray whom He wills and guides whom He wills. And you will surely be questioned about what you used to do." 16:93

"Indeed, those who have divided their religion and become sects - you, [O Muhammad], are not [associated] with them in anything. Their affair is only [left] to Allah; then He will inform them about what they used to do." 6:159

s.hukr

Noor upon Noor

Having disagreements with others should not be the reason why hate enters your heart.

Just because you disagree with someone about something, shouldn't be the reason why you abandon that friendship.

It's okay that you don't meet common ground. It's not a reason to be rude, to be selfish, to show ill character.

It should not be the reason why we push people away. Learn to defuse a situation with your excellent character. It's not your job to make sure everyone you meet has the same mindset as you.

Be open minded enough to let people express themselves even if you believe them to be wrong.

s.hukr

Noor upon Noor

Parents these days are not very
good at parenting. Trust me I know.

Too many young people share their
problems with me and 80% of those
problems occur within the house.

I'm not here to point fingers,
I'm here to share the reality.

s.hukr

Noor upon Noor

If you had not committed great sins on this earth, God would never reserve a place for you in Hellfire.

s.hukr

Noor upon Noor

A women's primary purpose is not to go outside and get the bread for the house. It is not her responsibility to earn like a man. Rather a women's weakness is the Dunya.

Her primary purpose is to maintain and establish her domain within her household.

She is the Queen of the palace so to speak. Her duty is to her household, her husband, and her children. She must meet those duties with good regard and only then, can she consider establishing herself outside the household.

s.hukr

Noor upon Noor

You need to stop putting yourself down,
You need to learn to love yourself,
You need to educate yourself,
You need to read the Quran,
You need to improve and grow,
You need to be strong and smart,
You need to be sincere and loveable,
You need to forgive yourself and move on,
You need to glow up,
You need to give yourself time,
You need to be physically fit and mentally able,
You need to forbid evil and encourage good,
You need to be wise and humble,
You need to be a True Muslim.

Not for me, but for yourself because you desire Jannah. I know you can do it because Allah said so.

You will be questioned on Yaumil Qiyamah about the time you spend in this Dunya. So start preparing yourself.

s.hukr

Noor upon Noor

Oi Muslim!

Please stop telling people your star sign, zodiac sign or whatever you call it.

It is Shirk.

Do you want to die a Kafir?

s.hukr

Noor upon Noor

I pray you find a someone whose soul clings to yours like you have known them for a thousand years. Someone who becomes a blessing to your eyes and guides you to the highest level of Jannah.

Say Ameen!

s.hukr

Noor upon Noor

Show me the most damaged parts of your soul
and I'll show you how you still shine like gold.

s.hukr

Noor upon Noor

Pointing out someone's flaws in public space whether it be in real life or in the comment section does not entail proper Dawah.

There is a correct way of giving advice. Sometimes that means completely ignoring them.

s.hukr

Noor upon Noor

"It's not Haram, where does it say
that in the Quran?"

Please stop using this excuse, it makes you
look stupid and arrogant. It doesn't have to be
stated in the Quran specifically for it to be
haram.

As Allah told us in the Quran, to the follow
teachings of the Prophet ﷺ in chapter 4 verse
59. Look it up yourself.

So if the Prophet of Allah said
it is Haram, it is Haram.

s.hukr

Noor upon Noor

Let me ask you the following:

School and University prepares you for what?

To make money? To busy yourself in the pursuits of worldly matters? To enjoy the temporarily pleasures of life?

To buy material things in the hope that it fills the void in your soul? To have bread on the table?

Is that all this life means to us?

What kind of knowledge is that? What kind of lifestyle is that? Are we not Muslims who live our life according to the ways of Islam?

So why are we living the lifestyle
of the non-Muslims?

s.hukr

Noor upon Noor

Muslims don't celebrate Christmas,
new year's or birthdays.

But hypocrites do.
Know the difference.

s.hukr

Noor upon Noor

I've met a lot of people in my life, but I don't like most people I meet. I don't care how rich, pretty or intelligent you are. I don't care about your social status.

My heart likes the company of those who are conscious of Allah. Not the judgemental type or those with a skewed perception of reality but those who are gentle, kind and soft inside.

Their presence makes me feel blessed and happy, the way they think, the way they behave isn't like normal people,
its pure and prestige.

They are wise enough to be humble and strong enough to tell the truth, never in a manner that would hurt you.

I meet them once and I already know they are different from the rest. It's like I met a person from Paradise.

s.hukr

Noor upon Noor

Nowadays, I find people to be afraid
of themselves. They have forgotten the
duty that one owes to oneself.

The duty of self-love, self-respect
and self-learning.

s.hukr

Noor upon Noor

This Ramadan, may the Angel on
our right keep writing and writing.

s.hukr

Noor upon Noor

I faced hardship early in life, it aged
my soul but beautified my heart.

God answered my wishes
I used to cry over.

Alhamdulilah.

s.hukr

Noor upon Noor

I'm constantly learning new things, exploring new experiences, pushing my limits because God didn't create me to be useless.

He made me to be the best of creation.

s.hukr

Noor upon Noor

If you're a Muslim and you start a
conversation saying hey or hello.

I'm going to block you.

Say Assalamu alaykum or Salam,
it's more soothing to my soul.

s.hukr

Noor upon Noor

The teacher is always silent during
the test and every student has the
potential to get the highest mark.

Some just never try their absolute best.

s.hukr

Noor upon Noor

People are delusional.

They expect you to read their mind and give them exactly what they desire. I find them strange because they expect from the creation, not from the creator.

They misplace their trust and hope in people. Only to become hopeless, heartbroken, and depressed until they realise what they desire lies only with Allah and they should only seek it from Him.

s.hukr

Noor upon Noor

If you're getting almost everything that you desire in this world without much struggle.

Then you must ask yourself is Allah giving me my reward in this life and reserving my punishment in the hereafter?

s.hukr

Noor upon Noor

Not everything is about you.

This world doesn't revolve around you.
You are not the centre of attention.
You are nothing but a speck of dust.

The more you crave attention the more
insignificant you become to me.

s.hukr

Noor upon Noor

It's funny how I notice Muslims buying from luxury brands. Temporary things that will not help in the hereafter.

They fall into this idea that if I buy from brands like LV, Gucci or Mercedes. They will be seen as successful, rich and beautiful.

But in reality, majority of them miss their 5 daily prayers, are insecure about how they look and financially dependent on others.

Isn't Salah our path to success?
Isn't Quran the way we beautify ourselves?
Isn't charity how we get richer in the eyes of Allah?

s.hukr

Noor upon Noor

Don't follow every advice or lesson. Use it as a guide to come to your own conclusions.

s.hukr

Noor upon Noor

Don't believe everything you hear.

Always do your own due diligence.

s.hukr

Noor upon Noor

If you hear of my death, make Dua for me.

Ask Allah to forgive and pardon me for all my sins. Ask Him to have mercy on me and to make my grave a good resting place. Ask Him to grant me a safe passage to Jannah.

s.hukr

Noor upon Noor

The life is this Dunya starts to become boring every time I start to read about Paradise.

s.hukr

Noor upon Noor

When we follow Islam,
our belief in Allah increases, we
become more blessed, educated,
righteous and more in control
of our life.

And when we don't follow Islam,
we allow disbelief to enter our hearts.
We stop seeking knowledge, we allow
our tongue to lie, backbite and do evil.

We allow disbelief to enter our hearts such
that we may describe ourselves as a hypocrite.

s.hukr

Noor upon Noor

What is friendship?

A true friend is someone who understands your perspective. Someone whom you trust to share your personal matters.

A person who loves you enough to not support you when you are wrong but is always there when you need them.

No distance of time can separate you from them. They want what is best for you in accordance with Allah, not their own self-interest or your own self-interest.

They give you good advice and constantly remind you of Allah. They want to see you succeed in life.

s.hukr

Noor upon Noor

May the angel of death arrive when you and I become the most righteous. May he come during the month of Ramadan.

s.hukr

Noor upon Noor

Don't hold back compliments it could make someone's day, while you earn a good deed.

s.hukr

Noor upon Noor

I don't like this generation.

We fight over petty things,
over temporary things.

The men are half the problem
and the other half are the women.

Instead of complaining about
each other. Learn to understand
and appreciate each other.

s.hukr

Noor upon Noor

The scars on my body have healed, they don't bother me. But the scars on my heart are sewn with fine thread.

Sometimes people say things they shouldn't and the thread breaks.

Pain overflows and tears start to flow. So I carry myself back to Allah in the hope that he may mend my heart again.

Be careful of your tongue.

s.hukr

Noor upon Noor

"You can't water the rose of a stubborn garden".

You can't force religion; you can't force
faith and you definitely can't force love.

s.hukr

Noor upon Noor

I don't like religious people.

They will push you away from Islam, make you feel bad for not practicing Islam and will embarrass and judge you in public.

But I love righteous people.

They pull you closer to Jannah without even making you realise it. They actually help to put you back on your Deen in the most loving and compassionate way. Their moral compass starts to influence yours just with their presence.

They are like a magnet that pulls you closer towards real beauty, love and peace.

Those are the real Muslims that I love.

s.hukr

Noor upon Noor

The older you get the more you really want someone with Eman in their heart, a warm smile, arms that hug you into comfort and when you look at them, you are reminded of how blessed you are to be with them.

s.hukr

Noor upon Noor

There are only a few things you NEED in life:

- Air
- Water
- Food
- Shelter
- Clothing

Everything else is just desire. The world runs on Desires not Needs. **Think about it.**

s.hukr

Noor upon Noor

Hijab makes you look confident, beautiful and you feel like royalty. There are so many benefits to the Hijab and I always admire Queen energy.

I know this world makes it difficult to be modest and to feel beautiful. But that's part of the test of this Dunya.

Allah made Hijab compulsory.
There must be wisdom behind it.
The harder the Hijab is for you,
the greater the reward from Allah.

Maybe you're not ready, but at least put some effort towards it by purchasing some Hijabs. Trying them on, with time, I'm certain Allah will make it easy for you.

Show Allah that you are willing to change your entire wardrobe for His sake. You want to enter Jannah, right?

So keep trying your best.
I pray Allah makes it easy for you.

s.hukr

Noor upon Noor

Next time you think someone is flirting you,
ask yourself if kindness is so rare in your life
that you mistake it for desire.

s.hukr

Noor upon Noor

When you realise the power of words,
you'll start to say less and
choose your words carefully.

When you realise the power of thought,
you won't waste time overthinking.

When you realise the power of influence,
you won't surround yourself with just anyone.

s.hukr

Noor upon Noor

People forgive but not with their whole heart. They forgive but then close their heart towards that person.

The poison of one's crime remains in their heart and fuels ill emotions towards the other.

If you really want to forgive, then do so with your whole heart. Forgive that person as if you have forgotten their crime. Clean your heart of all anger and hate.

Because when Allah forgives us, He does not punish us, he doesn't remind us of our short comings, instead he wipes away our sin and replaces them with good deeds.

s.hukr

Noor upon Noor

Sometimes I make a simple mistake just to see how people react and to reveal the true nature of people.

Then accordingly, I distance myself from the toxic ones and become closer to the good ones.

s.hukr

Noor upon Noor

Muslims attacking Muslims.

My heart aches at how nasty
we become in a blink of an eye.

Perhaps this is another test
from Allah to see who is who.

s.hukr

Noor upon Noor

I don't think I'll ever fall in love with
this world. I've already seen the ugly
truth behind the fake curtains of
perfection.

I dream of Paradise.
I hope I'm allowed inside and
if I'm not, I pray someone's
Paradise isn't complete
without me.

s.hukr

Noor upon Noor

Allah is so merciful, so loving and so just. That He sends down trials and tribulations in this life for the sins we have committed, to protect us from the punishment of the hereafter.

s.hukr

I heard Allah's Messenger AS saying: There is nothing (in the form of trouble) that comes to a believer even if it is the pricking of a thorn that there is decreed for him by Allah good or his sins are obliterated. - Sahih Muslim 2572g

Noor upon Noor

Some have ended their journey at 25 and are not buried until 75. Others will live multiple lifetimes within a single lifetime.

How would you like to live your life?

s.hukr

Noor upon Noor

If I were to thank Allah for a
thousand years, it would still
not be enough.

I hope these tears that come
from my heart, the ones that
are full of shukr are
heavy on the scales.

s.hukr

Noor upon Noor

Man is forgetful and man is weak
except the righteous who fear God.

Those are the successful.

s.hukr

Noor upon Noor

"Why is life so confusing?"

It's not. You never took time to
understand the book about life.

"Which book?"

The book written by Allah,
the one who created life.

s.hukr

Noor upon Noor

A man's shoulders were built for responsibility. He works all his life to fulfill that responsibility.

He is a giver, he gives from his wealth, his time and his mind. He maintains the order of his family, provides for his family and spends on his family.

Not only his family but also he is responsible for playing a part of his community.

Being a man is no easy task. But it becomes extraordinarily difficult when his own family becomes a burden on his shoulders.

The biggest burden a man can face is a wife who doesn't obey, who doesn't listen, while he has not done an ounce of injustice to her.

But has provided for her all necessities and given her the best of his ability. Such women are cursed by Allah.

s.hukr

Noor upon Noor

Why is everyone so selfish now?

I feel people don't take friendship seriously anymore. I feel that the reason we become friends with someone is not aligning with our faith.

People become friends with you for a benefit or seek friendship because they feel lonely even if that friendship is bad for you spiritually.

I miss the good old days when friendship was based on the aura of their soul.

We made bonds with people who we could help or provide mutual benefit, knowing that this person has a good heart, or this friendship may inspire goodness within the community.

s.hukr

Noor upon Noor

I know deep down your hurting. You try to control yourself but somehow tears fall down without you realising. You don't understand why it's hurting so much but it does.

Let those rivers fall, let your heart clean itself because it is about time you look inwards.

You need to reflect upon yourself, and if you still can't find peace, carry yourself to Allah. Verily, it is He who mends the heart.

s.hukr

Noor upon Noor

One of man's greatest joy is a reliable speedy horse. Even nowadays they measure it with horsepower.

But the horse that lies in his heart, has only one saddle. That is man's greatest joy. Not everyone gets to ride that horse.

s.hukr

Noor upon Noor

When you meet new people, pay close
attention to what they ask you and
how they ask you.

I find most people are not interested
in you, but in your temporary attributes,
like your wealth, your status, your beauty
and in your education. They are selfish,
they only focus on how you can help them.

They focus on stuff that doesn't matter,
stuff that doesn't describe the condition
of one's soul.

It's rare when I meet people that they aren't
concerned about this life because they have
already fallen in love with the next.

s.hukr

Noor upon Noor

If you understand the laws of God and the fundamentals of Life, you will start to live life very differently to everyone else.

Because now you know what is right and what is wrong, you understand what is important and what is not. You know exactly what to do and what not to do.

You'll start to live life like a
traveller on a journey.

s.hukr

Noor upon Noor

Growth is in the most difficult
decisions that you need to make.

Struggle is the price you pay for
every decision you make.

Stupidity is making the same
incorrect decision again.

Eman is a guiding light towards
success, peace, and prosperity.

s.hukr

Noor upon Noor

She showed me her beauty and expected
me to approach her, but I turned a blind
eye and ignored her.

She came back and said, "Am I not beautiful?"
so I said, "Yes, you are beautiful, but God
has reserved me for someone else,
you are not mine to look at."

She walked away confused as if she never
faced rejection before. Pondering at how
she still had respect for a man who told
her "No".

I later found out that she had converted
to Islam. When they told me about her
story, they said, a faithful man reminded
her of God in such a way that she cried
all night until she found Islam.

s.hukr

Noor upon Noor

80% of single Muslims have someone
they would like to marry but are
afraid from rejection.

I thought Muslims only fear Allah.

Why are we scared from something that is
halal? Go and get to know them. Engage
with them for the sake of Marriage.
So you can complete half your Deen.

This is your sign to either get married
or to move forward with your life.
Either commit to it or let it go.

Make a decision. Quit wasting
your time overthinking it.

s.hukr

Noor upon Noor

Either be a Muslim or don't be one.

Simple.

Don't play this game of being a hypocrite.
Don't play around in this world having a
fake label on your head that says "Muslim".

s.hukr

Noor upon Noor

You can dress attractively to your
hearts content but only for your spouse.

You are not allowed to be
immodest in-front of others.

You must be careful of your dress
code as it has direct relationship with
the respect you might receive.

s.hukr

7 Steps to help you face difficult situations:

1. Salah:

Make sure you stick to praying on time – 5 times a day. Never miss salah and do your best to pray each Salah with sincerity as if it's your last prayer in this world.

2. Read Quran:

Quran is so beautiful that no matter what difficulties you face you'll find solace in it. Read it carefully with understanding.

3. Make Dua:

The Dua for removing anxiety: "O Allah, I take refuge in You from anxiety and sorrow, weakness and laziness, miserliness and cowardice, the burden of debts and from being over powered by men." - Sahih al-Bukhari, 7/158

4. Give Sadaqah:

Give lots of charity, as much as you can, because it helps push away hardship. And if you can't give money, even kind words or a smile will do.

...

5. Set Goals and Have Vision:

Don't let Shaytan play with you and keep replaying the video of your hardship in your mind over and over again, move on! Set new goals, new projects, and remember you're with Allah, nothing should stop you!

6. Wake up Early:

Wake up before Fajr and work on your ideas and projects, or simply read Quran. Getting busy before daybreak is a definite way to move away from your hardship and overcome challenges. Get most of your ideas/work done in these early hours.

7. Hardship is Not Lost:

Remember, Allah will never forget the injustice and hardship you faced, so don't worry about seeking revenge or trying to get justice.

Keep knocking on God's door until He changes your fate. Not according to your best interest but according to whatever is best for your soul.

s.hukr

Noor upon Noor

Never hurt a heart full of love,
because if it breaks, that heartache
may turn into a curse that will follow
you to your grave.

s.hukr

Noor upon Noor

It depends how blessed or cursed you want to be. You already know that there are plenty of things you could be doing to improve your connection with Allah.

To improve the condition of your heart, your body and soul. However, Shaytan's whispers get to you. Therefore, stopping you from reaching your true potential in life.

Allah doesn't burden us; Allah doesn't want us to be miserable or depressed or cursed.

There are people who put 1% into self-improvement and others who put in 110%.

It's all on you and how desperately you want to change yourself.

s.hukr

Noor upon Noor

I just wanna build my empire now.
Help people as best as I can and leave
this world better than how I found it.

s.hukr

Noor upon Noor

We all like to believe that Allah would allow us into His Paradise. That He will show us mercy and forgiveness. And Yes, He is the most merciful and forgiving.

But some of us will never smell the fragrance of Jannah, some of us do not deserve Jannah, because we simply do not follow Islam.

We are insincere with God.
So prepare for His Wrath.

s.hukr

Noor upon Noor

Whenever life has tested me with something
and I passed the test, God has always
rewarded me with something.

Sometimes, He bestows knowledge by
teaching me a lesson and sometimes
He gives me a gift. I prefer the Gift.

s.hukr

Noor upon Noor

Love people in such a way that your love is pure. It is not a desperate or needy type of love, nor does your love vary by how much someone loves you back.

Love people purely for the sake of Allah and watch how your love, with time,
travels to their hearts.

s.hukr

Noor upon Noor

The root cause of depression and anxiety is caused from a fear of something other than Allah. Fear of no rizq, fear of losing a loved one etc.

Having strong Eman gives us the understanding that all good and bad thing comes from Allah and that everything belongs to Allah.

When you have firm belief that Allah should be the most feared and that for every hardship comes ease. Hope will naturally enter the heart and you will never feel depressed or anxious.

s.hukr

Noor upon Noor

If you make my heart smile,
I'll melt your heart until
it flows like honey.

s.hukr

Noor upon Noor

I don't like it when people praise me.

I much rather they spend time thanking Allah. Praising me will just feed my ego and I want to stay humble.

Thank Allah instead. For He is the one who guided me to you.

s.hukr

Noor upon Noor

If you look at the people in your circle and you don't get inspired, you don't have a circle. You have a cage. I suggest you run away.

s.hukr

Noor upon Noor

"God has gifted every woman the
patience of 10 men and during
pregnancy she gains the ability
of 10 more men."

s.hukr

Noor upon Noor

Sometimes, all I want is to go to the house of Allah. Forget about everything and focus on what really matters. I'm not tired of this world, I'm just tired of the people of this world.

Because when I spend time with people of the Quran, I feel like I'm amongst people of Paradise.

Are you from the people of the Quran?

s.hukr

Noor upon Noor

As soon as you reach the age of adulthood, you cannot be friends with the opposite gender outside your immediate family, at least not how the west portrays it.

This is to protect each other from Zina.

It doesn't mean you cannot communicate or socialise with each other, but it must be with Haya, respect and in public light.

Only talk if there is something that needs to be discussed or there is genuine purpose.

There is wisdom behind it.

s.hukr

Noor upon Noor

I am not a teacher to
teach you anything.

God has gifted you a
mind, hands and feet.

Use them as best as you
can and when you get
lost, raise your hands
and talk to God.

And in your heart let
there be hope, because
God always responds.

s.hukr

Noor upon Noor

Kind loving words makes a woman's heart move but ever wondered what makes a man's heart move?

s.hukr

Noor upon Noor

Sometimes you meet people and they just
enter your heart without any permission, as
though they have reserved their
place a long time ago.

s.hukr

Noor upon Noor

A woman's greatest hardship is this Dunya and to conceal. To conceal her blessings, her beauty, her speech. To keep the trust that she has been given by Allah.

A man's greatest hardship is to lower his gaze, to endure a difficult life and to continuously serve his family and his ummah according to the instructions of Allah.

s.hukr

Noor upon Noor

If you are a true Soldier of Allah,
nothing will scare you, not even death.

Because you live and die purely
for the sake of Allah.

s.hukr

Noor upon Noor

There is a hidden world of
Kings and Queens and Lovers.

People that live up to their gifts,
they live their best lives by pushing
themselves towards Greatness.

I always admire such people because
this life is not kind to them.

s.hukr

Noor upon Noor

A man works all his life for what?
To acquire wealth for himself?

No. He works hard not for himself but for others. His shoulders are heavy with the responsibility to provide, protect and lead a generation of people.

Yet some men come to a house not a home, a witch not a wife, hardship not ease. And people wonder why he left for the milk and never came back.

s.hukr

Noor upon Noor

Turn your calamities into festivities
and your faith into a weapon.

Be so close to God, that if you wish a
thing, He always grants it to you or
gives you something better.

s.hukr

Noor upon Noor

There was once a King. Nobody knew his name and he didn't care.

When I asked him why? He told me that God knew who he was and that was enough for him.

s.hukr

Noor upon Noor

Girl if he can't listen to the whole
khutba, what makes you think he will
listen to you talk about your problems?

s.hukr

Noor upon Noor

As long as we stay divided
under nationalities created
by the west, we will suffer.

Only when we choose to
unite under God's book.
Only then will we triumph.

s.hukr

Noor upon Noor

Please don't disturb my peace. If you have something to say, don't. Tell God instead.

s.hukr

Noor upon Noor

I miss the old days when life
was simple and love was plentiful.

Common sense was common and
people knew in their heart what was
right and what was wrong.

Now, it only gets worse with time.

s.hukr

Noor upon Noor

It is not the dress that I find attractive.

It is your modesty. It's not the makeup that makes me smile, it's the Noor glowing from within you.

I wish you understood this.

s.hukr

Noor upon Noor

Be the soul that follows the right path that isn't easy, but it is the most rewarding.

s.hukr

Noor upon Noor

I appreciate kindness. I appreciate those who ask me if I'm okay. I appreciate every person in my life who has tried to brighten my day and succeeded.

s.hukr

Noor upon Noor

A true Queen never claims to be a Queen
and a true King never claims to be a King.

Don't tell people how good you are or
what you do, don't go outside your way
to show off your wealth, your status and
whatever Allah has blessed you with.

Stay hidden, for gems are meant
to be hidden in plain sight.

s.hukr

Noor upon Noor

Love has no language boundaries.
Love has no borders.
Love doesn't discriminate.
Love doesn't care how rich or poor you are.

True love overcomes many obstacles,
but you must be willing to **sacrifice**.

s.hukr

Noor upon Noor

The mosque is free of charge
but mostly empty.

The clubs and shisha lounges
are paid but mostly full.

It's free to earn Jannah and
expensive to earn Hell.

s.hukr

Noor upon Noor

There is no wealth like intelligence,
no poverty like ignorance and
no inheritance like good manners.

s.hukr

Noor upon Noor

How to impress any Woman:

1. Maintain a strong connection with Allah
2. Learn how to cook & dress well
3. Be great with children
4. Be mentally and physically fit
5. Have good speech
6. Never lie
7. Have Haya
8. Have ambitions & goals
9. Be protective but not insecure
10. Knowledgeable in Deen & Dunya

s.hukr

Noor upon Noor

How to impress any Man:
1. Be God Conscious
2. Not be a Feminist
3. Be emotionally intelligent
4. Be great with children
5. Not be clingy or insecure
6. Knowledgeable in Deen
7. Obedient
8. Hijab & Haya
9. Is playful
10. Makes great food

s.hukr

Noor upon Noor

Women desire 2 main things,
one is respect, the other is love.

If you don't love her, she won't
leave you but if you don't respect her.

She will definitely leave you.

s.hukr

Noor upon Noor

Salam,

I know this might be random,
but I hope you have an amazing
day full of blessings and that Allah
guides your beautiful soul towards
Paradise.

Don't let the temporary enjoyments
of this Dunya get to you because I
would really like to meet you in
Jannah one day.

s.hukr

Noor upon Noor

Can we normalise saying السلام عليكم to
other Muslims instead of Hey or Hello.

Make it so normalised that even
Kafir say Salam instead of Hello.

s.hukr

Noor upon Noor

I firmly believe that every person has a gift from Allah. Some are blessed with creativity and some with an analytical mindset, some are naturally lucky, and some are talented in other areas.

But each and every one of us is born with a potential for greatness deep inside us. It is very sad that many of us spend our whole life unable to reach our true potential and are withered away by meaningless worldly pursuits.

s.hukr

Noor upon Noor

Happiness was asked: "Where do you live?"

It replied: "In the hearts of those
content with Allah's decree."

s.hukr

Noor upon Noor

A woman who loves and supports
you when you have nothing, she
deserves everything and more.

s.hukr

Noor upon Noor

The same way you go to the gym
to build up physical health is the same
way you go to the library to
build up mental health.

These days you don't even
need a library, almost everything
can be accessed from a few taps
on your phone.

For how long will you stay miserable
because of your lack of awareness.

Allah doesn't burden a soul more
than he can bare, but sometimes
you burden yourself more than you
can bare by not following Islam to
the best of your ability.

s.hukr

Noor upon Noor

Be careful of who you call your friend.

They will influence you over time. If you accompany yourself with wrongdoers, your likelihood of becoming like them increases exponentially.

s.hukr

The Prophet ﷺ said: "A person is on the religion of his companions. Therefore, let every one of you carefully consider the company he keeps." - Tirmidhi

Noor upon Noor

Some people chase
success but I never did.

I never wanted to be rich,
famous or anything.

I liked my simple lifestyle.
However, success was chasing
me while I was chasing Allah.

My life changed once I
understood the beauty
behind God's words.

s.hukr

Noor upon Noor

Being humble, wise and sincere.
Now that's attractive.

s.hukr

Noor upon Noor

As a man, you are the leader, the breadwinner, the one in charge and the one with responsibility. The one accountable for your family.

Your job isn't to lead according to what your wife says or what your father says, their job is to advise you as best as they can, not to control you or to make decisions for you. Allah appointed you to make the final decision according to the principles of Islam.

Your job isn't just to earn Rizq for your family, you must also be present in the upbringing of your children, ensuring the next generation continues to excel in Deen and Dunya. Your children will be a reflection of you, so you must push yourself towards greatness. You will be an example for your children.

You must spend time and energy on your marriage, with your wife, invest in your marriage so it doesn't crumble into heart break. It's not about money, it's about time, communication and sacrifices. Establish a deep understanding with her and help her, support her, be there for her. She is your wife. The mother of your children.

s.hukr

Noor upon Noor

Don't be that man that is cursed by Allah because he neglected his responsibility upon his wife, his family, and his Deen.

Pleasing people is an impossible task. Instead, spend your energy pleasing the Almighty and watch how your life changes overnight.

s.hukr

Noor upon Noor

Towards the end of every year, I like to reflect
upon my life. Do a recap of what happened
and what didn't. Ponder about the new people
I met and people who have left me.

Go over significant events that have
lead me to the path I am on today.

And check if I have achieved the goals
I have set for myself or did my goals change?
Am I getting to where I want to be?

I keep asking myself questions to determine
my progress. Because if I die tomorrow, I
want to have lived a lifestyle that I would
be happy to die upon.

s.hukr

Noor upon Noor

Why do you think that a good heart is someone who doesn't pray? A heart without hijab and a heart who overthinks, a heart without the remembrance of Allah.

How can it be good? Tell me!

That's not a good heart, that's a heart filled with doubts and fears.

Why do you allow Shaytan to brainwash you into thinking that your heart is good when half the time you feel empty inside?

Hopefully, there might be some light in you, so use that light and recognise the true condition of your heart so that you can do something about it.

s.hukr

Noor upon Noor

A good heart has peace within, tranquillity
and love pouring down like a spring.

A good heart doesn't neglect or disobey Allah.
A good heart is someone who lives life
according to the true nature of Islam.

Living a lifestyle dictated by God.

s.hukr

Noor upon Noor

You can't be successful in Deen
without Dunya. Neither can you
be successful in Dunya without Deen.

You need both as a Muslim.

A True Muslim is someone who
strives for the best in worldly matters
while establishing himself firm in faith.

Faith is a component of your character, your
ethics, your principles and morality. It is what
makes you different from the non-Muslims
but also the reason that excels you in Dunya.

s.hukr

Noor upon Noor

Your reaction to hardship is what determines how much money you will have. How strong your relationships will be and how strong your Eman will be.

Hardship itself doesn't determine your life story. God wants to see how you handle the test questions of life. Now read that again.

s.hukr

Noor upon Noor

Be happy in whatever stage of life
you are. Accept your reality but also
try your absolute best.

Be grateful for everything and
enjoy whatever life brings your way.

Last I checked, a Muslim doesn't stress
over worldly things, we stress over the
matters of the hereafter.

s.hukr

Noor upon Noor

If you are rich, spend
time with the poor.

If you are righteous, spend
time with those who are not.

If you are young, spend
time with the old.

If you were raised in the west,
spend time in the east.

You won't understand the other
side of life until you go exploring.

s.hukr

Noor upon Noor

People love to blame their mistakes and flaws on everyone except themselves.

I call those people toxic.

s.hukr

Noor upon Noor

I'm convinced that age doesn't matter,
it's your ability to adapt to different
people of different ages. Sometimes
you need more patience and sometimes
you need more love.

Age is just a measurement of how long
you have lived. It doesn't define your
status or character or anything else
important. Don't give it so much weight.

s.hukr

Noor upon Noor

Your diet has a huge role to play
on your body's health and well-being.

It affects your mood, your ability
to stay active, your behaviour, your
skin, your mental health.

"If you eat like an animal then
you become an animal"

Modern day sickness such as
high blood pressure, heart attack,
cancer etc are partly due to one's diet.

So eat that which is good for
you, and fast from time to time.

That is better than to be
stuck in hospital.

s.hukr

Noor upon Noor

The Root of all diseases is within our heart.
The love and attachment to this materialistic
world stems from our heart.

We know this world is temporary, yet we
find it so hard to disengage from it.

May the Almighty guide our hearts into
desiring what is lasting - the Hereafter.

Remember, the life of this world
is merely enjoyment of delusion.

s.hukr

Noor upon Noor

Some people are so precious.

They deserve more than your heart.
They deserve your Duas at Tahajjud.

s.hukr

Noor upon Noor

Many of you have yet to win
the war inside of you.

For as long as you allow overthinking,
worries, doubts, fears, and insecurities
to plague your heart and mind.

You will remain weak in my perception.

s.hukr

Noor upon Noor

Idk who needs to hear this but stop developing feelings for people outside of marriage.

Takes max 2 weeks to get to know someone and 1 week to get married, not 8 months and then I'll think about out.

or 5 years and I'm heartbroken and it's not my fault. You attract and repel people based on who you are, not who they are.

s.hukr

Noor upon Noor

Are you slave of money?

Are you a slave of the school system?

Are you a slave of your ego?

Are you a slave of what people
think about you?

Are you a slave of materialistic desires?

Are you a slave of your emotions?

Are you a slave of your job?

Are you a slave of things other than Allah?

If you said **Yes** to any of them,
you are committing shirk.

s.hukr

Noor upon Noor

Prioritise people over worldly things.
It might be a Dua that saves you from
the hell fire.

s.hukr

Noor upon Noor

I am at peace knowing that God's greatest work happens in the most impossible situations.

s.hukr

Noor upon Noor

Please don't criticise someone in front of everyone. Make that conversation private.

Hide sins, hide mistakes, don't expose them.

s.hukr

Noor upon Noor

I talk about love and people
assume I'm in love.

I talk about Islam and people
assume I'm a sheikh.

I talk about money and
people assume I'm rich.

I talk about women and people
assume I'm misogynistic.

I talk about knowledge and
people assume I'm smart.

Why can't I be free to talk about anything without
you declaring your assumption about me?

You don't even know me.
I never asked and I don't wanna know.
I don't care. Keep it yourself.

God knows who I am and
that's all that matters.

s.hukr

Noor upon Noor

Some people will never change,
no matter how much you care.

s.hukr

Noor upon Noor

I live in a world where the bare
minimum is treated like gold.

s.hukr

Noor upon Noor

Thank you for reading this book.

I hope that you enjoyed it and found some benefit from my words.

May Allah always have mercy on you and guide you towards the straight path. **Ameen.**

Sincerely,
s.hukr

P.S If you love this book, please promote them and share it with others and maybe you'll earn a good deed and guide someone towards Jannah!

P.S.S If you loved this book, you should checkout my other books.

fajrnoor.com

S.hukr Books

1. Fajr and Noor

2. Through His Eyes

3. Noor upon Noor

4. Slice of Paradise

5. Mumin Mindset

6. How to Marry a Muslim Girl

7. Divine Love

www.ingramcontent.com/pod-product-compliance
Lightning Source LLC
Chambersburg PA
CBHW030255010526
44107CB00053B/1724